On My Best

Behavior

For More Booklets...

Interested in more copies of *On My Best Behavior* to share with others? Each of the booklets in the *Me, Too!* series is available in packages of five.

Looking for guidance on every aspect of developing inclusive preschool strategies? The complete set of all six booklets in the *Me, Too!* series will provide you with extensive techniques for enhancing children's early years.

Contact Brookes Publishing Co. at *410-337-9580* or *1-800-638-3775*, or visit our web site at *www.brookespublishing.com*.

To write to the publisher: Paul H. Brookes Publishing Co., Post Office Box 10624, Baltimore, Maryland 21285-0624, U.S.A.

Typeset by Integrated Publishing Solutions, Grand Rapids, Michigan.
Manufactured in the United States of America by H & N Printing & Graphics, Timonium, Maryland.
Cover art and interior illustrations by Lori Esposito.

The *Me, Too!* series is based on research conducted through the Early Childhood Research Institute on Inclusion supported by Grant #HO242K4004 from the U.S. Department of Education, Office of Special Education Programs. No official endorsement by the federal government should be inferred.

Parent quotes and case scenarios are from actual people and events. In all instances, names have been changed; in some instances, identifying details have been altered to protect confidentiality.

Library of Congress Cataloging-in-Publication Data

Hanson, Marci J.
  On my best behavior / [Marci J. Hanson, Sonya Gutierrez Matias, and Maria L. Morgan].
    p.   cm. — (Me, too!)
  ISBN 1-55766-513-3
  1. Handicapped children.   2. Preschool children.   3. Behavior modification.   4. Child rearing.   5. Parents of handicapped children—Handbooks, manuals, etc.   I. Matias, Sonya Gutierrez.   II. Morgan, Maria L.   III. Title.   IV. Series.
HV888 .H37 2001
649'.64—dc21   00-068924

British Library Cataloguing in Publication data are available from the British Library.

Baltimore • London • Toronto • Sydney

Introduction

Chances are, if you're reading this booklet, you have a child between the ages of 2 and 5 years. It's a time of new experiences and challenges for children and their parents. As a parent, you are accustomed to making decisions to help your child grow, develop, and learn in appropriate ways, but now, you will also be deciding how to help your child belong and participate in school and other community activities. Will your child make friends? Will your child know how to behave? Will your child be able to do the things the other children are doing?

This booklet is one in a series called *Me, Too!*, designed particularly for families of young children with disabilities. Although these booklets are written directly to parents and other family members, teachers, child care providers, and other professionals will find them valuable, too. Plan to pass these booklets back and forth among the adults who are important in your child's life. Here is a brief description of each booklet:

Introducing Me: This booklet is different from the other booklets because it is one that you create. You fill out the pages to tell others about your child. Share this booklet with your child's teachers and with the other professionals and caregivers who work with your child.

It's Time for Preschool: This booklet helps you learn more about selecting a preschool for your child, connecting with teachers and other families, knowing what the law guarantees you, and making the early school years a positive experience for your child.

My Community, My Family: This booklet helps you learn about building good relationships between your family and others in the community. You will find good advice on locating appropriate, accessible programs and activities. Strategies also are included for making activities meet the needs of all children.

My New Friends: This booklet explores ways that you can encourage friendships between children. The importance of friendships is highlighted through suggestions designed to help your child develop friendships with classmates and make new friends in the community.

On My Best Behavior: This booklet will help you understand your child's behavior. You will learn techniques to help you support positive behavior, discourage negative behavior, and avoid behavior problems by planning ahead for new situations.

Look What I Can Do Now: This booklet focuses on introducing strategies for modifying schedules and the physical environment to make it easier for your child to participate in programs and activities.

In each of these booklets, we will be talking about the term *inclusion*. Inclusion usually refers to the joint participation of children with and without disabilities in school and community programs and in activities. Although people may think of inclusion as something that only happens at school, inclusion is actually a very broad concept that refers to participation in many settings (e.g., child care, recreational programs, libraries, religious activities, athletic organizations, museums). In the most general sense, inclusion is about belonging. When a child belongs, he or she is a part of a group and has opportunities to join activities with other children. Inclusion is good for children.

We hope that the *Me, Too!* series will help you as you begin to develop inclusive strategies to meet your family's needs. You will find experiences and recommendations that other parents have shared with us to help you. We address issues and decisions commonly faced by parents and suggest strategies for you to consider when planning for your child and family. As you study these ideas, always keep in mind that you, as a parent, are the expert as to what works for your family!

On My Best Behavior

❝ *Oh, I'd love to see him in regular school and not talking so much to himself. It's kind of cute because he's little. But when he gets older, it's not going to be cute anymore. And people are going to ask, 'What's the matter with this kid?'* ❞

—Patrick's mother

We all want our children to belong, but we also want to celebrate their individuality. All children have different personalities, ways of communicating, and strengths and needs. As a parent, you have grown to love these aspects of your child that make her exactly who she is. Sometimes, though, differences can cause a child to be excluded from the group. Most preschoolage children haven't had much exposure to someone who acts or looks different. Young children often stare and ask questions the first time that they see people who walk or talk differently. This curiosity is normal, but children with disabilities may have a tough time fitting in, particularly when their behavior stands out.

Part of raising children includes helping them learn acceptable behavior and what is expected in certain situations. Sometimes, though, the rules are not clear or they are inconsistent; for example, different types of behavior are expected for dining at home, going to another family's house for dinner, and eating in a restaurant. Even within these categories, different behavior is expected—making a quick stop at a local pizza parlor or sandwich shop is different from spending the evening at a nice restaurant. Some children find it difficult to differentiate appropriate behavior in various settings and don't understand why a loud voice is fine in a crowded park but not in a movie theater.

This means that challenging behavior often cannot be categorized as either good or bad behavior, and all children have good days and bad days. As a parent, the key to working with challenging behavior is to have goals and develop a consistent plan to meet these goals. Look for the building block icon for special tips.

UNDERSTANDING BEHAVIOR

What Is Challenging Behavior?

It is difficult to define *challenging behavior* because acceptable behavior depends on the situation. As a parent, you know your child best, and you can identify consistently challenging behavior. Your child may test limits and challenge rules and authority. Perhaps she withdraws from groups or refuses to participate in certain activities, or perhaps your child is quite affectionate and accustomed to giving hugs frequently throughout the day. At home, you have encouraged your child to express feelings and show affection, but now that she's in preschool, the hugs she likes to give during storytime are disruptive and unacceptable. Talking to your child's teachers, care providers, or other people who spend time with your child will help you figure out the difficulties your child is having throughout the day so you can begin to think about how to address them.

What Causes Challenging Behavior?

All children are different, and the causes of challenging behavior are likely to be different as well. You can look for the causes of your child's challenging behavior by noticing when and how it occurs. Does a specific time of day or activity trigger the behavior? Is there a person or place that seems to consistently be involved? The amount or level of light, sound, colors, touch, or activity may cause confusion and stress for some children. Other stressful events that trigger challenging behavior include not knowing what is going on, major changes in daily routines, feeling unheard or unappreciated, and not knowing what to do next.

What Discourages Challenging Behavior?

As you try to determine the causes of your child's challenging behavior, you can also look for people, objects, and situations that discourage this behavior. Does a special toy calm your child? Does a favorite person help encourage your child to participate in the group? What helps your child understand new situations? When children's behavior is challenging, it is just as important to understand what prevents or discourages the behavior as it is to know what causes it. For example, if talking about feelings discourages your child from hitting others, then she needs to have time to talk. If your child is confused by the amount of activity around him, then limiting chaotic activity or creating an alternative activity may be helpful.

What Is the Purpose of Challenging Behavior?

Behavior has many purposes. Its most basic function is to communicate and express feelings. If your child's behavior is challenging, she is probably trying to tell you something. Is your child hurt or upset? Is he tired or hungry? Does she want to avoid doing something? It is important to identify the cause and purpose of your child's behavior so the adaptations and plans that you make will be appropriate.

Can Adaptations Be Made to Encourage Acceptable Behavior?

Once you understand the causes of challenging behavior and what your child is trying to tell you, you can make changes to encourage acceptable behavior. Sometimes, a place or an environment is unsettling to a child, or the boundaries of what is acceptable are unclear. Perhaps the environment can be adjusted or changed so that it is less stimulating. Noise, music, and activities can be reduced. You could try giving fewer choices or defining them more clearly. Sometimes, too many children are involved in an activity or the space is too small, too large, or not properly set up. If children have to sit too close together or don't have enough room to move around the circle when they play Duck, Duck, Goose, they may not be able to concentrate on the game. If the area in which children gather for storytime is too big, other things in the room may easily distract them.

Is There a Plan for Addressing Challenging Behavior at Home and School?

It is important that you know how discipline is handled at your child's school and how children's behavior is managed. Ask administrators and teachers about their educational philosophy to find out if it meshes with your family's beliefs. You, as a parent, have the right to be part of the planning and decision making necessary to meet your child's needs. Developing a clear-cut plan to manage challenging behavior helps you and your child's caregivers provide consistent strategies at school and at home. Rules that change according to the situation and methods that are different from day to day can be confusing and work against encouraging acceptable behavior.

CREATIVE SOLUTIONS

Because the types of challenging behavior are often quite different depending on each child's personality and situation, you should think of the following strategies as suggestions. Be creative as you modify them, and build a plan to best fit your child's needs. Collaborate with your child's teachers and care providers, and get their input on any ideas you may have.

Using Transitions to Anticipate Change

" *[We] tried a private preschool last time, which did not work out. We were asked to leave….* "

—Tehra's father

Beginning a new preschool program can be difficult for young children. Change, itself, is stressful or upsetting for some children, especially when it comes as a surprise. Transitions between activities give children time to prepare for change. Transitions that indicate what will happen next make your child's day go more smoothly. Planning ahead, developing rituals, and preparing for change can help alleviate your child's anxiety by systematically introducing new activities into relaxed, stable environments.

[A] *Plan for change.* When you develop consistent daily schedules, changes are easier to handle. Without a regular daily routine, little changes occur frequently throughout the course of each new day, making big changes confusing and difficult to manage. Use the following tips to plan for changes in your child's daily routine.

- Write down your child's typical daily routine: waking up, getting ready for school, eating meals, going to school, attending after-school activities, and going to bed. Also, think about subroutines in your child's day. Bedtime, for example, is only part of the daily routine, and many steps may be involved: bathing, dressing for bed, brushing teeth, reading, and so forth. Your child has many routines!

- Based on your child's daily activities, establish consistent, comfortable routines at home and at school. This will help your child more successfully navigate busy times.

- Talk about the routines with your child as you reach different daily activities so your child can anticipate what comes next.

- Try to limit major or abrupt changes in your child's schedule, and remember to be as consistent as possible. A regular routine will help your child better understand your expectations and allow your child to cope with surprises.

[A] *Develop rituals.* Subroutines or consistent rituals that accompany specific activities help establish positive behaviors and create transitions among daily activities such as eating, going to school, bathing, and sleeping. These rituals signal the next activity in the daily routine and bring completion to the previous one.

- Instead of engaging in rough and tumble play before bedtime one night and then playing Hide-and-Seek the next, establish a quiet bedtime routine to use every night (e.g., brush teeth, put on pajamas, read a story, say goodnight, turn out the light). Once you establish a particular order to this kind of ritual, you'll be surprised by how quickly your child will notice if you miss a step or go out of order.

- Use a particular task or establish a consistent habit to signal specific events during the day. Ask your child to help set the table, put ice in glasses, or wash his hands to signal the transition to mealtime.

- You may have difficulty getting your child to eat or sleep when she is still thinking about playing with a toy, and establishing rituals can help focus your child's attention on the activity at hand.

[A] *Establish a routine.* When new events or activities are added to the daily routine and your child is given plenty of advance notice, changes can be more enjoyable for everyone involved.

- Encourage your child to talk through the daily schedule with you. Once you have had a chance to show your child how to describe the day, see if she can do it all by herself. Prompt your child with questions such as, "What do we do after breakfast?" or "What happens after we get home from school?"

- Take your child on trips to practice anticipating change and to develop strategies to cope with change. If he will soon begin a local museum art class, get your child ready to go and make several trips to the museum at the same time that the program begins. Try to take these trips on days when your child is relaxed and most likely to easily handle the trip.

- Slowly integrate changes by adding them to your child's established routine. Integrating each step of a new routine will help your child make the transition more easily. For example, you could start by getting your child ready to go out a few times, then getting her ready for a trip to the museum without going into the classroom. After she is used to this routine, get your child dressed, take her to the museum, and then visit the classroom.

If your child's preschool class is going on a field trip, introduce the idea to him well before the activity and talk about things your child may see on the trip. Tell your child that it is all right to be excited and to try something different. Assure your child that he can rely on the support of family, teachers, and classmates. You may even want to practice the activities planned for the field trip ahead of time with your child and family.

Practice Positive Behavior

66 *We joined a swimming club and take her there. She plays with younger kids there. Her personality draws kids to her.* 99

—Maya's mother

Challenging behavior occurs less often if you develop your child's interests and help your child practice positive behavior. When you encourage positive behavior, your child begins to understand what kind of behavior you like. By reinforcing the behavior you like, you can help your child develop a habit of being good.

 *Build on your child's interests.* Plan activities that include your child's favorite things. If your child likes trains, let her explore a toy train. Visit a train or subway station and take a ride on a train. Allow opportunities for your child to play with trains with other children. Perhaps your child will share information about her experience with another child. She may want to invite a friend on a train ride, or your child may want to pretend that she is riding on a train.

 *Reinforce your child's strengths and abilities.* Give your child opportunities to shine by doing things that you know he can do. You might allow your child to be a leader or expert in an activity in which he is highly interested. For example, have your child tell the class all about dinosaurs and show classmates his collection of dinosaur books and toys.

[A] *Provide activities that encourage movement.* Exercise and movement benefit your child's health and physical coordination and can provide a terrific outlet for pent-up energy. Activities such as gymnastics or karate channel energies and provide opportunities to interact with other children. Organize a weekend walk with other parents in your community and their children. You could go hiking along a rural trail or sightseeing in a nearby historical or tourist area. You can also try organizing a family or neighborhood clean-up day: Rake leaves in the backyard or sweep the sidewalks.

Support Social Interactions

66 *There are kids who are scared of him because he touches them in the wrong way. He pats them, but sometimes it hurts.* 99

—Marvin's mother

Talk to your child about possible answers or reactions to a specific situation. You might ask your child, "What should you do if someone starts playing with some of the blocks you have been using?" or "What should you do if you want to use a wagon but someone else has been using it for a long time?" Role-play with your child or ask a brother or sister or another child to practice social situations with your child. Mix fun scenarios with more serious situations to keep the role play interesting.

Try an arts or crafts activity with a group of children. Encourage them to share and take turns using materials. Discuss alternatives to outbursts, and praise positive efforts and reactions so the children understand your expectations and how to act.

[A] *Learn to get along with others.* Getting along with others is perhaps the most important social skill that children learn. Because interaction is a regular part of our daily lives, helping children get along with people who aren't relatives or friends is crucial to their development.

- Create opportunities for children to model how to get along with others. Get to know the children who are class leaders or who include your child in their play. Ask them to share or talk with your child. When the children are playing well together, you can praise them for sharing and cooperating with one another.

- Arrange short play dates during which lessons on turn taking, sharing, and other social skills may be learned.

- Support your child and other children in their play. Let other children know how best to talk and play with your child. Help your child learn social gestures or manners such as saying "Hi" or "Good-bye" and taking turns.

You may want to invite one of your child's friends to play after school or on the weekend. The children can practice social skills, and you can feel comfortable that you are within arm's reach to supervise.

[A] *Express feelings positively.* Part of interaction includes making others aware of how we feel. Young children often act on their feelings without explaining the reasons for their actions. This kind of behavior can be confusing to other children.

" *Billy was playing with several toy cars. Nasheeka thought that he was only playing with the car in his hand, so she picked up one of the cars and walked away. This angered Billy, and he pushed Nasheeka. Because Billy never communicated reasons for his actions, Nasheeka became confused.* "
> —Nasheeka's father

To help your child develop ways to interact positively with other children, try the following methods:

- Encourage your child to express how he is feeling. Observe your child's emotions and ask questions to help your child think about different feelings.

- Encourage your child to let you know when she is angry, hurt, or frustrated and to explain why.

- Give names to different feelings, such as *sad, lonely, surprised,* and *excited*. Show your child how feelings are expressed through words, gestures, tears, and so forth.

- Use pictures to help your child label how he feels. A "thermometer" to measure emotions can be helpful. Together with your child, you can look at a picture and identify how happy or sad or mad your child is feeling.

- Develop a calming down strategy so your child can have some time to deal with his feelings. Some calming down strategies include counting to 10, taking deep breaths, and learning to walk away.

- Have scripts that provide alternative reactions to a certain situation. Ask your child, "What do you do when someone calls you a name?"

You could also encourage your child to talk about and draw his options for behaving. In this drawing, a child could depict three things that he can do when, for example, his sister makes him angry. Your child might determine that he can 1) stop what he is doing, 2) ask for help, and 3) tell his sister that he doesn't like what she is doing.

Catch Your Child Being Good

❝ *He's very vivacious and outgoing. He's a good kid. He's a fun kid, because he's active. His mind is going all the time.* ❞

—Mickey's father

Most of us enjoy being acknowledged for our hard work or something that we have done well. Children are no different. If your child is outgoing and active, tell her you like that quality. You can spare yourself a lot of unnecessary discipline by making sure that you practice ongoing positive reinforcement. Don't forget to praise your child for appropriately behaving at home. Here are a few examples of praise and positive reinforcement:

"I like how you used your quiet voice."

"I like how you asked politely and said, 'Please.'"

"Thank you for putting your cup down on the table so gently."

Children also need practice interacting appropriately with other children. You can help your child learn expected behavior by being attentive to positive behavior:

"You shared so nicely with Roberto."

"I like the way you waited for your turn."

"Cassy likes the way you hugged her gently, not too tightly."

You'll be surprised how much your child likes to be "caught being good." Praising children helps them learn positive behavior, but it also prevents them from developing a negative self-image. Although discouraging negative behavior is often necessary, reinforcing positive behavior, as well, will help your child say, "I was good today because...."

Redirection: Find Another Option

66 *[At the grocery store], you better be prepared to buy her something, because she'll yell and scream and carry on at the top of her lungs until she gets it.* 99

—Michiko's father

Although parents would rather not yield to children's demands, sometimes it seems easier than dealing with challenging behavior. Because parents often want to avoid making a scene, they ignore some of the less conspicuous problem behaviors. When overlooked, though, behavior, such as hitting, throwing a tantrum, or grabbing a toy, may escalate into even more challenging behavior. It is often easier to redirect behavior when it is first noticed than have to react later to a full-blown incident. Allow your child to find other options and other things to do.

If your child grabs another child's toy,

- Say, "Let's see what *you* can play with" or something similar.
- Introduce another activity.

If your child wants a snack before mealtime,

- Ask your child to help prepare the meal and "taste the cooking."
- Serve a small portion of the meal as an appetizer.

If your child wants a toy or candy that she can't have at that particular time,

- Give a choice between two activities. Say, "Would you like to read a book or color a picture?"
- Promise the candy after a specific goal has been met. Say, "If you help me finish shopping by staying by my side, you can have the candy on the way home."
- Ignore the request.

Change the Space and Environment

66 *Unfortunately, we found that some caregivers and day care providers have a hard time with him…because he is a high energy type of kid.* 99

—Alphonse's mother

Caregivers and teachers may be unwilling to work with some children because of their behavior. Support the child and prevent challenging behaviors from occurring by creatively changing the surrounding environment to meet her needs.

A *Set rules and boundaries.* Rules should be simple and clear; for example, say, "We do not hit other children" and "We take turns." Rules should be consistent and direct, and explanations should be limited to what a child understands.

- Be firm with boundaries. It is easier to stay within the rules when the child knows them well. Provide opportunities for your child to practice following the rules. Have some flexibility, but don't stretch established boundaries.

- Establish regular appropriate consequences. Children need to learn that actions have consequences. Be consistent to help children learn what is not acceptable and what happens when their actions are not acceptable. Consequences should be appropriate for the behavior. For example, if a child tears pages out of a book, he will not be allowed to use the book. Think about consequences in advance rather than at the height of the situation to be sure they are fair and not based on anger. It is not very effective to give unrealistic punishments or ultimatums such as, "I'm never going to let you play at the park again!" It is more effective to say, "Throwing sand is not allowed. It hurts other children. You have to leave the sandbox now and come back when you are ready to play nicely."

- Provide opportunities for your child to play with other children. Children learn a lot of rules about playing and talking with each other when they play with some support from adults.

🅰 *Adapt the environment.* Adapting the environment effectively requires sensitivity to a child's individual needs and can help decrease problem behaviors. Try these suggestions:

- Observe what triggers your child's challenging behavior, and adapt the environment to limit these triggers. For example, if your child starts screaming when there is a lot of commotion, decrease the amount of noise and activity so that the environment won't seem so chaotic to your child.

- Provide more activities and choices to capture your child's interest. For some children who react to not having enough activity in their environment, these activities and choices will discourage challenging behaviors.

A PLAN FOR RESPONDING TO CHALLENGING BEHAVIOR

Although it would be nice to eliminate your child's challenging behavior, this isn't a practical goal for young children who are growing, learning, and testing their limits. Although much of this booklet focuses on ways to discourage the frequency of negative actions, it is also a good idea to develop a formal plan for responding to your child's challenging behavior. The following behavior plan incorporates many of the strategies suggested to discourage negative behavior. Use Max's plan as a template for your child's plan.

Behavior Plan

Date: *May 25*

Child's name: *Max*

Child's age: *4 years*

Challenging behavior: *Throws tantrums during shopping trips*

When and how it occurs: *During family trips to the store, Max cries until he gets what he wants.*

How we react to the behavior: *Feeling embarrassed and buying a toy or candy or leaving the store*

Beliefs or feelings that may discourage progress: *Continuing to feel embarrassed and buying toys or candy*

Goal: *To decrease tantrums in public*

Plan:

1. *Before going to the store, tell Max where we are going and what is expected.*
2. *Tell Max what will happen if he has tantrums in the store: I will say "No, Max," and we will leave the store.*
3. *Be firm about expectations and consequences.*
4. *Practice expectations and consequences at a nearby store when we are not in a hurry. Tell Max "No," and leave if he has a tantrum. It is important to follow through with consequences.*
5. *Praise and encourage positive behavior (not tantrums). Example: "Max, you waited for Mommy so patiently," or "I like the way you looked at that toy and then put it back on the shelf."*
6. *To prevent tantrums, let Max bring a favorite toy or book along to the store. The toy or book will give him something to do during shopping trips. Playing with the toy or book is incompatible with tantrums.*

Date: *July 10*

Progress: *Max is able to go to the store without tantrums at least half of the time. Max is able to play with toys or books and remain occupied for at least 10 minutes on shopping trips.*

As you think about creating a behavior plan for your child, use the following suggestions, which are designed to make planning and responding to your child's challenging behavior less complicated:

- Identify your child's challenging behavior.

- Observe when and where the challenging behavior occurs.

- Talk with your child's preschool teacher or caregiver about which approaches work and don't work with your child. Develop consistent strategies to manage your child's challenging behavior.

- Develop an intervention plan with your child's preschool program team. Specific behavior goals and strategies can be written in your child's individualized education program (IEP). Strategies and responsibilities should be clearly stated, and the plan should be consistently implemented both at school and at home.

YOU CAN DO IT!

Although the suggestions outlined in this booklet will probably not eliminate all challenging behavior, following these recommendations will help you manage your child's inappropriate or unacceptable behavior. Remember: Identify challenging behavior and its causes; establish daily routines and rituals; concentrate on encouraging positive behavior; anticipate change and make adaptations to help your child; and above all, don't forget to praise and encourage, hug and smile, be patient, give space, and say "Great" or "Nice try" to acknowledge your child's progress.